RETURNING TO FREEDOM

BREAKING THE BONDS OF CHEMICAL SENSITIVITY AND LYME DISEASE

DUKE TATE

ISBN 978-1-951465-01-8 MOBI
ISBN 978-1-951465-02-5 EPUB
ISBN 978-1-951465-00-1 paperback

Pearl Press, LLC
PO Box 2036
Del Ray Beach, Florida
33483

This book is dedicated to my Sufi Guide and doctor, Ali Dede (www.sufismo.com), who patiently attended to my health over the years and got me 100 percent well of my ailments.

CONTENTS

LYME DISEASE

My high school was a very prestigious boarding school in Connecticut, in a gorgeous lush green valley down from the Appalachian Trail with a wild river flowing right beside the campus. One afternoon in 1999, during my senior year at boarding school, I was clearing paths on the Appalachian Trail for my mountain biking team—punishment for cutting practice—and I got bitten in the navel by a tick, though I didn't even feel it at the time. It wasn't until later that night when I was sitting at my crunched desk studying that I suddenly felt the sensation of something in my navel. I lifted my shirt and was horrified at the sight of the engorged tick, right in my belly button. I raced to the infirmary to have it removed. The nurse said it was a wolf tick, so I couldn't have been infected with Lyme disease. I went back to my dorm room that night feeling relieved, but a few days later I had the typical bull's-eye rash around the bite, which itched and is common to Lyme. Lyme was discovered in East Lyme, Connecticut, so I was well within the area of influence.

A week later, I developed flu-like symptoms that persisted for two weeks, time which I spent racked with chills in the infirmary. Still, they refused to treat me on the basis that I was bitten by a wolf tick. At the time, I was smoking pot and cigarettes occasionally, which were both strictly against school policy, and I was scared to press the issue. I thought for sure, as any paranoid young deadhead might, that I would be expelled—that they would be suspicious and drug test me and find marijuana in my system. I was so naïve back then. If Lyme disease is caught quickly, it can be treated in two weeks with antibiotics, but if left untreated, the spirochetes go deep inside the body where it takes a long time and massive doses of antibiotics to kill them. Some people never recover.

Spring semester of senior year in high school, I

trudged along. After the bite, I felt off—I was weaker and tired a lot. I smoked more and drank more caffeine to have energy.

Graduation day rolled around on the first of June 1999. I was in the old stone Saint Joseph's Chapel with my sweet parents, Ken and Charme Tate, who had flown up for the celebration. My father, Ken, was an architect with a very well-established firm in Jackson, Misssissippi, and my mother, Charme, was an interior designer with an office in his firm. That day in the chapel surrounded by my parents and fellow students, I suddenly had difficulty breathing and was exceptionally thirsty. I quickly left the chapel and sat down outside alone on a stone wall to catch my breath. I stayed there until the end of the service. When my parents came outside, they were very concerned about my well-being. I told them I was faint and short of breath, but I would be okay. So, we plowed on through the festivities.

As my parents were leaving to return home to Jackson, they were still visibly concerned about me. I told them not to worry, but inside, I too was worried. What was wrong with me? It had been months since the tick bite, and I had all but forgotten about it. I wanted to push through and go to the legendary senior parties with my friends. Boarding school kids weren't allowed to smoke, kiss girls, drink, go out at night, watch movies, or do, really, anything at all, so after graduation, all that pent-up mischief erupted into a free-for-all.

During the senior parties, everyone was drinking a lot. Some people were hooking up. A cute blonde classmate with aqua eyes came up to me, pinched my butt, and wanted to make out, but I couldn't care less. I wanted to celebrate and party, but I just felt so bad. This was not like me at all. What was this?

By the final party, I was just barely hanging on. I couldn't wait to go home.

I had left for boarding school my sophomore year in high school due to depression and partying too much by my own choice. I asked my parents to let me. That first year away from home, starting in the fall of 1996, was very challenging for me. I missed my friends and was quite sad about being away from a girl I had a massive crush on back home, even though she didn't reciprocate my feelings. My diet was also terrible. I would skip meals and then feast on whole pizzas. I lived on soda; I smoked cigarettes in the bathroom when I could and dipped Skoal tobacco in my room, spitting into empty soda cans.

I did become very good friends in Connecticut with a large group of guys, and by senior year, the girl in Mississippi was a distant memory. I became close friends with a girl named Stephanie from South Carolina who shared my obsession with spirituality. We had long talks on life and God. In time, I fell in love with her, but I was always too shy to tell her how I felt.

Still, even with Stephanie in my life, high school was a bumpy ride for me, full of potholes. I was a major hippie, and during the spring of 1999, I decided to turn my short red hair into dreadlocks. I kept getting caught smoking cigarettes and I frequently cut class, although I somehow managed to make pretty good grades and did well on the SATs. For all my intellectual abilities, I was a true underachiever. I probably could have gone to Harvard or Yale if I had cared at all. But nothing really mattered to me besides spirituality and jam bands—a form of improvisational rock n' roll centered around long periods of free-form playing. The most popular jam bands are the Grateful Dead and Phish, but groups like Dave Matthews Band and Widespread Panic also do it. I had, in fact, already decided by the fall semester of my senior year that I would not be going to college the next year; instead, I would hit the open road to follow Widespread Panic as they toured from city to city across the USA.

On the airplane ride home to Mississippi from Connecticut, the altitude and compressed air in the plane made it truly difficult to breathe, and I was also extremely thirsty—thirstier than I had ever been in my life. I probably drank two gallons of water before arriving in Mississippi later that night. My head felt like it was in a vice; I was pale and felt faint.

I told my mother about my symptoms when she picked me up at the airport, and quite naturally, she was very worried for me. My mother, a warm woman raised in north Mississippi by a good spiritual family, had always supported me through my ups and downs. It was a relief to be at home under her care, though I was still scared. I thought I might die. The next day, we went to an urgent care clinic where the doctor insisted I had the flu and sent me home. We decided to wait it out for another two weeks, even though we both knew it wasn't the flu.

My whole family had been deeply involved

with alternative health since my grandfather had used certain techniques to help my mother with her systemic candidiasis in the 1980s. *Candida* is a genus of yeast common in a healthy body that can overgrow when there is a lack of healthy bacteria in the digestive tract. When it develops into candidiasis, the infection can enter the bloodstream and cause extreme fatigue and many other bizarre symptoms. My mother was cured of hers through juicing, homeopathy, and various nutritional supplements (which I will refer to as "nutrients" from here on) after being unwell for some months. Dr. Seneca Anderson, a holistic homeopathic doctor in Atlanta, Georgia, had treated her on my grandfather's recommendation. My grandfather, Irwin Tate, who was close to Dr. Anderson, had severe muscular degeneration due to radiation poisoning from viewing the atom bomb tests in Los Alamos, New Mexico, in the 1940s as part of his service in the medical corps of the National Guard. All his friends who had been at the test had died or were very ill. This had prompted him to search endlessly for good health practices that could stop the degeneration. Since the tests, he had worked out rigorously, eaten well, and eschewed sugar, alcohol, and cigarettes—attributes that were quite unusual for a man of the 1950s. On his quest, he had found Dr. Anderson many years prior to my mother getting candidiasis and had even bought him a dark field microscope useful for detecting *Candida* yeasts.

When we felt overlooked by the clinic, my mother decided to have me send a blood sample to Dr. Anderson, which he subjected to his Vega test —a bioenergetic regulatory machine that has its origins in acupuncture and homeopathy. The Vega test scans the body or blood for abnormal electrical charges, which indicate a certain virus, bacteria, parasite, or toxin. Using the Vega test, Dr. Anderson found indications of meningitis in my blood sample, and so he shipped me homeopathic drops and nutrients for that. The Vega test could find an illness like meningitis that was present at a low level in the body without being acute due to the body's immune system not reacting to it. I was very ill, and the treatment didn't make me feel much better. There was a little healing reaction that I was so hopeful would lead to a cure, but it didn't.

I was supposed to go to a Widespread Panic concert in Morrison, Colorado at the famous Red Rocks Amphitheater, with two high school buddies of mine at the end of July, 1999. I had fallen in love with the soulful music of this jam band from Athens, Georgia, and the irony of the band's alarming name given my terrible physical state was completely lost on me.

I had still never seen them play live, like all my friends from Mississippi had, because I was always at boarding school when they were playing in my home state. I had bought tickets for the show at the end of the school year, assuming I would be well by July. When the time rolled around, for some godforsaken reason, I decided to force it and go. We planned to be gone a week. My buddies— Matt and John—drove my mom's navy Volvo station wagon the whole way. I sat in the back, chugging quart after quart of water and feeling like hell. I went to the bathroom so much I would pee in Gatorade bottles rather than asking them to stop. When we reached Morrison, I felt so bad that I stayed in the hotel room while Matt and John went to the show the following day. Normally, I would have been so sad about missing the show and hearing my first live renditions of "No Sugar Tonight" or "Greta," but I felt so ill, I didn't even care. My head felt like it was in a vice, I couldn't breathe at all, I had extreme thirst, my neck, body, and muscles were all very sore, and I was fatigued to the point of exhaustion.

We made the long journey back to Mississippi, but I had finally realized and accepted just how sick I was—and it was clear from my steadfast attitude during the trip that there would be no willing myself to wellness without some medical intervention.

The rest of 1999 passed slowly as my symptoms got increasingly worse. Mom knew about a healer in Florida named Casey who could perceive things about people's health from a distance, so she called her and had her take a "look" at me. Casey stated that there was a bug in my head, possibly a spirochete, and I needed the antibiotic Rocephin to get well. Her diagnosis sounded right, so we went to a doctor and begged for Rocephin, telling him about the tick bite. He reluctantly agreed to give us a few shots. I couldn't see that they made much difference, so we didn't try anymore. What a mistake that would prove to be.

My symptoms worsened to the point that I had trouble traveling in a car. Movement caused my head to feel compressed and tight, and my breathing grew shallow. I stayed in my parent's house, bedridden save for a little light walking around the house, mainly in my room. Every day was a struggle.

One day, Mom brought home some chicken salad atop chopped greens from Swenson's restaurant. San Francisco-based Swenson's was my favorite place to eat in Jackson, so I was game for the food. You may know this joint from their ice cream popularized in the famous movie *The Goonies*. Anyway, I got very ill with diarrhea after eating the food. Mom and Dad were fine, so I knew I had been susceptible to a bug due to my immune system being compromised. I could not stop going to the bathroom; finally, I got so weak that my parents checked me into one of the biggest hospitals downtown. There, the doctors ran lots of tests for bacterial infections and other issues they thought might be causing my stomach and other strange symptoms. The tick bite meant nothing to doctors in Mississippi in the late 90s, and I was not given any test for Lyme. All the tests came back negative for everything. Back then, Lyme disease was considered by allopathic doctors in the South to be a small tick-borne illness treatable within two weeks of infection and isolated to the northeastern part of the United States.

My chronic diarrhea continued, so the doctors

finally prescribed me an antibiotic for giardia, a microscopic parasite, just based on my symptoms.

One night in the hospital with my mother, Charme, sleeping quietly over near the window, I had the most vivid dream. I was walking in a heavily wooded forest when I came to a fork in the road. Up ahead on one path was an old friend of mine from boarding school whom I had admired because he was smart and all the girls liked him. All along the path were thousands of white plastic straws. I then looked to my left, where there was another path made of earthy wooden tiles. At the end of it stood a white wolf with brilliant blue eyes, staring at me. When I woke, I immediately told my parents about the dream; my father and mother were amazed by the symbolism. They said I needed to have it interpreted by their Jungian depth psychologist, Ken Gilburth, because it seemed profound. I resisted because I was scared of talking about my past with a therapist, but after some coaxing, I decided to have a telephone consultation with him.

Within two days, the antibiotics had cured the giardia. And I was released and sent home with no treatment for my strange Lyme symptoms. Some-time that week, I spoke to Ken Gilburth, the therapist, who proved to be a kind, gentle man with a strong Appalachian accent. He did a brilliant dream interpretation, informing me that I had come to a fork in the road of my life. The path of straws represented the path of the world, and my friend waiting for me was "of the world." The other way, the path of the white wolf, was a spiritual path waiting for me. It was of the earth and real like wood. I loved Ken's interpretation and set up another appointment with him a week later.

I watched movie after movie after movie to pass the time while lying in bed as we tried to figure out what to do next. I read also, mainly spiritual books. My spiritual journey had started my senior year in theology class with Father Beck when we discussed free will. When I mentioned it to my father, he told me there was no free will, really. People, he explained, only behaved in ways they were conditioned to behave, so what was free about their decisions? He told me about a mystical teacher named Gurdjieff whose works he had read in college and who taught people to develop their beings and decondition their thought patterns. Right when I heard about this mystic, I knew I had found a spiritual tradition that was unlike anything I had yet encountered in my life.

In my parents' upstairs den where I stayed bedridden on a fold-out sofa, I decided to take the first plunge into Gurdjieff's teachings. George Gurdjieff was a Russo-Armenian mystic who emerged as a spiritual teacher in Russia, France, and America in the early part of the twentieth century. Dad gave me *In Search for the Miraculous* by P. D. Ouspensky and I read it quickly because the characterization of mankind as being asleep and having to make efforts to wake up and become conscious of a higher reality deeply resonated with me. The book was full of interesting mystical knowledge. I moved on from that work (which I would later learn was Sufi in nature — Sufis were the bridge between all religions and their path represented a way to God through the self-realization of Truth) to other traditions: Shamanism and Carlos Castaneda. And now, I was talking with Ken once a week via the phone because I was still too ill to travel to his office in Jackson, Mississippi.

All the while, I was having very lucid dreams. My attention to them seemed to make them increase in frequency. Ken and I were doing traditional psychotherapy for my past, and dream therapy as well. During this time, I would also go outside on the upstairs porch of our Charleston-style house to sit and try to meditate.

My grandfather Irwin Tate had been following my health journey very closely. He had also been a bodybuilder and got into nutritional supplements in the 1960s before anyone else was taking them. He mentioned he had a chiropractor named Scott in Palm Beach, Florida to my parents and I, who used applied kinesiology—a method of testing the body through resistance for nutrients. We managed to travel to Florida to see him, though the trip was very hard on me. Dad pushed me through the airport in a wheelchair. Scott was a tan, laid-back California type with a long ponytail. I got on his chiropractic table, where he tested me by placing a Spirulina capsule in my hand and pulling my arm down while I resisted. He put me on six or seven nutrients and said he would check me again in a few months. I don't remember what the other nutrients were except I do recall shark cartilage being among them. After several months, he traveled to Mississippi to retest me and put me on different nutrients. He said I should be well in a few months, but my condition had not improved at all. I highly value his practice of applied kinesiology, but for whatever reason, the nutrients didn't help me much. By this point, I had stopped trying to get treated for Lyme disease. No one in Mississippi would even test me for it, and I was too ill to travel to the Mayo Clinic or anywhere else.

Shortly afterward, my family and I moved from Madison, Mississippi, to Covington, Louisiana (on the north shore of New Orleans), to expand my father's growing office. Dad was now working outside of Mississippi in Nashville, Tennessee and Kentucky on much bigger jobs, and he wanted to work nationally. To do so, he needed to be near an international airport, which New Orleans had. He had also started the first monograph on his work with New York graphic designer Oscar Ojeda, which would go on to be published by Australia-based Images Publishing, one of the largest architectural book companies in the world.

Once in Louisiana, my mother reluctantly drove me to Columbus, Mississippi, to be treated by an alternative MD who had worked with my grandfather Irwin. While there, I felt so ill from traveling in the car that I had to be hospitalized. That week in the hospital was full of mainstream tests that all came back normal; the doctors thought I was a hypochondriac.

Mom and I returned to Louisiana and

continued to try alternative therapies. After many months of various treatments, we met a registered nurse who worked with an MD who agreed to take on my case. From my symptoms and the bite in Connecticut, he was willing to diagnose me with Lyme. He prescribed three months of the antibiotic Rocephin intravenously and three months of oral Cipro. Insurance wouldn't pay for it, though—we would have to pay the $85,000 out of pocket. And so my parents paid for it. What choice did we have?

About five months after the first antibiotic, I felt well enough to drive again. The antibiotics were working, but it was a very slow climb to getting back out in the world again physically. I had lost a lot of muscle strength in my legs from lying around all day. I progressed so slowly I didn't notice much change from one day to the next.

I moved to Asheville, North Carolina, to be near another homeopathic doctor who had had success with Lyme.[1] I rented an old brownstone within walking distance of downtown, which was just magical. Snow fell from the heavens on the wintry days, chimney smoke was always in the air, and there were lots of organic cafes. Asheville was a cozy and warm place with good vibes all around.

My mother was an interior designer, so she and I bought lots of cool antiques and big comfortable sofas and chairs for my place. She stayed in my second bedroom for three months until I felt secure being left alone. Then I lived on my own.

I was better, but I still just felt bad all over. I started smoking cigarettes again—a habit I had started when I was fourteen, trying to be cool. I also drank caffeine to feel better. I did eat organic and mostly only ate healthy foods, but I didn't know about nutrition, detoxification, or juicing. Like my father, Ken, who had always suffered from hypoglycemia (low blood sugar), I reacted terribly to refined sugar at that time and began eating a pretty strict high-protein and low-carbohydrate diet.

Dr. Pete, my homeopathic doctor there, did help me some with my symptoms, but it was painfully slow. After a year, I decided that continuing the treatment was not productive and that I would move to Nantucket in Massachusetts to write a book about the enneagram—a personality typing system I had studied with my parents since childhood—while doing the best I could to manage my health.

The enneagram system was developed by

Gurdjieff and was Sufic in origin. It states that there are nine essential personality types among humanity, each type corresponding to one of the "passions," or Christian sins (the seven deadly sins plus deceit and fear). Every type had a "wing" and three subtypes of which a person could be one: social, one-on-one, or survival. Fifty-four types of people existed when the wings and subtypes were included, which made the enneagram rather diverse and complex. My parents and I found it to be a way of deeply understanding ourselves, friends, and strangers. I had always dreamed about being a writer since reading many of Shakespeare's plays at school in Connecticut, and so I thought I would try to write a book about the enneagram.

I moved to the beautiful whaler's island off the coast of Cape Cod in the fall of 2002. Since my childhood, I had been enthralled with the cold northern waters of the Atlantic. I had envisioned a life off the coast of Massachusetts or Connecticut in some sleepy fishing town where it snowed and was gloomy at least part of the year. Never a day of sun—that was my idea of happiness. I was looking for a place like Seattle but didn't know it at the time. Maybe I had seen too many Stephen King movies growing up, practically all of which were set in Maine, but I had an idea of what I wanted in my mind and was going for that 100 percent. I was looking for a geographical cure to my remaining symptoms, too. I still didn't feel well. I had to drink Diet Coke throughout the day for the caffeine or I would have zero energy, and I was smoking again for the same reason.

Nevertheless, I took a road trip in my steel blue Grand Cherokee along the coast of Massachusetts, visiting Salem, Gloucester, and Woods Hole. When I hit Cape Cod, I took the ferry to Nantucket and stopped there. I felt it was just my kind of place.

I liked living there in many ways. I would go out and drink at the bars in town every now and then, and play pool with the locals. I didn't even care about drinking that much. It made me feel exhausted and exacerbated all my symptoms. I mainly hit the bars as a way to meet friends.

I still ate healthfully during this time period. My favorite Nantucket dish was New England clam chowder. That cold-water seafood always felt so good for my body. Meanwhile, I started to write a book about the enneagram. I was particularly fascinated by how certain enneagram types looked almost identical to one another.

However, around that same time, my neck pain, which I had always experienced from the Lyme disease, got very severe. I went to a doctor, but he simply put me on pain pills, which I despised. They made me feel like I had just landed on the moon and was bouncing around in a space suit. I couldn't stand that altered feeling.

My neck was very rigid and would make popping sounds when I moved it. It was always sore, so I decided to return to Louisiana and stay with my parents until I could figure it out. An osteopathic doctor took an MRI of my neck and said the cartilage had deteriorated due to the Lyme bug and I would need to have the discs in my neck fused by the age of thirty. At the time, I was twenty-one years old. She prescribed some pain meds, lidocaine patches, and physical therapy. The physical therapy was not fun, but it helped the pain a lot. I was consistent and did it diligently while living back home in Louisiana. I truly missed Nantucket, though, and thought that when I was well again, I would move back to the sea, where I had always felt free.

From March 2002 to May 2003, I lived back home in Louisiana and read almost all of Idries Shah's books on Sufism as well as some of the various other titles published by Octagon Press. These writings, which struck me as a form of "real" Sufism, stated that the Sufi Way had existed since the time of Adam, albeit under different names. It was a bridge between all religions and expressed the inner essence at the core of each. When I wasn't reading about Sufism, I worked on my enneagram book, although that project had a short lifespan. My main interest in it was how the various types looked similar, and I wanted to explore this. I lost interest when there didn't seem to be any way to show or prove any of it outside of my own perception.

While living at home, my parents decided to open a design and art store in Fairhope, Alabama, where we owned two vacation homes. They said I could manage it and that a job might be good for my health. I agreed and was truly excited by the whole idea since I had always been a creative child and loved art. Also, I missed the water, and Fairhope was near the Florida border on the Mobile Bay, which I liked. There was lots of good seafood and it was an easy place to live at a nice slow pace.

As for my health, I didn't know how I felt. When I would try to work out with weights as I had done in high school, I felt so tired and lethargic. I still smoked a pack of Marlboro Lights every day and drank Diet Cokes one after the other to have energy. I didn't know what to do, so I just tried to live my life the best way possible.

I met Lexi during my first summer in Fairhope at a bar called The Raven Night. I was playing pool with my childhood friend and roommate Mathew and our next-door neighbor Maddox. Mathew went over to talk to Lexi and her friend, and Lexi told him how much she liked me. He invited them back to our house for drinks. At the house, I found out she was from Fairhope, but had just finished her freshman year at college in Memphis where she was an English major and a Kappa Delta sorority girl. We started flirting and the chemistry was very strong. She had beautiful curly blonde hair and astonishing blue eyes—I was very attracted to her. We could talk for hours with ease.

I stayed in the little town of Fairhope for the next school year before deciding to move to Oxford, Mississippi to attend college at the University of Mississippi. I wanted to be closer to Lexi as Oxford was only an hour's drive from Memphis. Summer of 2004, Lexi was living with me in Fairhope as she had the summer free from college.

We drove the eight hours up to Oxford together to find me a place for my freshman school year and I ended up renting a two-bedroom apartment on Old Taylor Road in Oxford, Mississippi.

The walls were that puke yellow color often found in cheap apartments, so Lexi and I decided to paint them. We bought all the Benjamin Moore paint and brushes from Home Depot and, trying to save money, decided to do it ourselves. The first wall in the living room went well, but after that I began to feel very fatigued. I didn't know what it was, but assumed I was allergic to the paint. What else could it be? I had experienced some mild allergies in my life and they had often made me fatigued, so this was not something foreign to me. Lexi and I went to a hotel for the night. The next day, I hired a local painter to knock out the rest of the apartment for us.

We took the long, slow drive south to Fairhope, Alabama, where we had planned to spend the rest of the summer anyway. I was living in a charming house I had rented the year before, right on the Mobile Bay. I didn't think too much of any of it at the time. When I returned to Oxford in the fall to move my things in, the apartment didn't bother me at all. But something had changed—in the back of my mind, I was thinking, "What if I can't tolerate being around fresh paint anymore? What if I have other allergies?"

Fall 2004 at the University of Mississippi started out well. I was twenty-four and it was my first time attending college, so everything was new and exciting to me. The Oxford campus was beautiful at that time of year. The Southern belles walked the square in their Umbros and Greek shirts, while the frat boys drove around in their Jeeps and trucks listening to Dave Matthews or Widespread Panic. It was always a lively scene. I had some good friends from my hometown in Jackson, Mississippi, who were finishing up undergrad, and some others who had just started at the law school. There was always something to do. A buddy of ours owned a house in downtown off "The Square" where he would host large parties. He had a hot tub, which was cause for some interesting moments. Lexi was three years younger than me. She would drive down for weekends in her old tan Toyota Camry, and we would all go out to cool bars on The Square. She was very pretty and sweet, and we had a lot of fun together.

2

THE REAL JOURNEY STARTS NOW

My freshman year at the University of Mississippi in 2004 went well enough. I was taking some para-legal classes, which I didn't like. I started to realize I would never be a lawyer; however, I loved my Chinese religion classes and film classes. I was smoking so many cigarettes and drinking so much caffeine—surprise, surprise, I still didn't feel well. I was wired from the stimulants and nervous all the time, but without them, I had no energy. I had never recovered my health. I kept going back to Dr. Anderson in Atlanta for his homeopathic cure for Lyme. The treatment (which involved taking homeopathic amounts of the Lyme bug diluted in a miniscule amount of alcohol under the tongue two to three times a day to initiate an immune response) helped a bit, but not much. I could remember what perfect health felt like when I was young, and I knew it now eluded me. That feeling drove me crazy. I just woke up feeling ill every day. I was always tired and my neck hurt chronically. I had also now developed eosinophilic esophagitis and erectile dysfunction. The ED was so embarrassing with Lexi because I was so young and there was nothing to do about it. After my grandfather died from a heart attack while he was on Viagra, I was too scared to take the blue pill.

In the spring, Lexi and I broke up after two years of dating. She had wanted to get married, but we had problems. I felt like she constantly flirted with other guys and would tell me about it to make me jealous, which bothered me. I was paranoid about her that way also. My anxiety had started when I was a young boy. With Lexi, I was always tired and had no vitality for a relationship, not to mention the ED ruined everything. I had also become sensitive to perfume and could now no longer wear cologne without coughing and draining. I assumed those symptoms were allergies. But they were chemical sensitivities like my paint sensitivity.

All my illnesses were piling up, and one night, I was so distraught that I decided I must find an answer to my problems some way, somehow. By this time, Google was gaining momentum and I had noticed I could do a search for anything and find some very valuable and uncommon knowledge. I went back to Gurdjieff and the Sufi Tradition. By this point, I knew these spiritually enlightened masters had answers about health and life that eluded ordinary people. I searched and searched the internet until I found a Sufi Institute operating in Mexico by the name of Instituto Alef. I read the website and knew I had found a place I belonged. The school offered a clear picture of its objective to transmit a path to enlightenment for the student using exercises from the Sufi Tradition that activated the spiritual organs of perception that lay dormant in the ordinary human being. The website went into detail about the use of the ninety-nine Attributes of God in Arabic in the heart, including the explanation that each person contained one such attribute as the primary one for them in their heart, called the *Sirr* or "the Secret of the Heart." The website was in English and had a Spanish translation as well and the Institute was totally Western in outward appearance, but used these select Arabic words and phrases because the sounds in that language itself are sacred and have a different effect on the heart and being than the English or Spanish counterparts. For instance, it is very different to say the word "Salam" with Intention from the heart than to say the English word "Peace" with Intention from the heart. "Salam" has the frequency of Peace as an attribute to it, whereas the English word "Peace" only echoes that state. Speaking the Arabic language unconsciously however, without Intention, has little or no effect on the spiritual state of a person, select phrases and words must be used sometimes in combination with Intention, certain breathing exercises, visualizations and/or head movements for the effects to occur. The Instituto's website themes and descriptions were so profound, they could only have come from the tongue of an enlightened man or woman.

That night in the spring of 2005, I wrote to the director of the Institute to apply to become a student. Ali Dede replied quickly and accepted my petition. He immediately began assisting me with my health, long distance from Mexico through email at that point. Dede had studied under Idries Shah and his brother Omar Ali Shah, and was a savant about health. One of Dede's teachers had operated a school for incurable patients, lived to be over a hundred and twenty years old, and even rode a horse at that age.

Ali Dede took a whole health history from me and then told me to cut out diet drinks and cigarettes right away. It was very difficult, but I did it. Dede also recommended I read Aajonus Vonderplanitz's book *We Want to Live*. This extraordinary book was divided into two parts. The first part was Vonderplanitz's own story about curing himself of blood and bone cancer and diabetes by eating raw foods, which included, all being raw: butter, cream, milk, eggs, cheese, honey, fruit and vegetable juices, salads, fruits, coconut cream, oils such as coconut and olive oil, and meats such as sushi and steak tartare. He also helped his son recover from a life-threatening illness with the same foods. The second part gave instructions for what foods to eat for certain ailments. The basis for the diet is that the destruction of enzymes in food can cause illness, and heating does this to food. The living enzymes in raw food, Aajonus claimed, not only healed the body, but detoxified it as well. In the book, Aajonus does have a theory about bacteria and viruses that is incorrect, which confuses so many people. He claimed such bugs are always beneficial as they feed on toxins in the cells and that process is a detoxification. While it is true that some bacteria like the kind found in unpasteurized kefir and grassfed raw milk contains very beneficial pro-biotics, and bad bugs do feed in the body, I believe now there are good and bad bugs and only the live enzymes in raw foods are responsible for the detoxification and rebuilding of the body. Any bad bugs are merely a by-product of an acidic cellular environment and a nuisance that must be done away with for a person to thrive.

After finishing the book, I immediately started making grass fed raw milk smoothies with raw organic fruits, flaxseeds, and unheated honey. I also started juicing raw organic vegetables and fruits. The detox from all of this began fast and hard, but every time I would go to the bathroom, I felt better afterward. Through this book, I also learned how certain chemicals could be obstacles to health as well. I started going to Wild Oats (a health-food store) and buying organic shampoo, soap, detergent, and cleaning supplies.

Dede recommended I take 1,000 mg of vitamin C and 500 mg of magnesium daily right away, but I didn't listen to him. Vonderplanitz's rigidity about supplements in *We Want to Live* had scared me off them. I should have known better. I should have listened to my teacher. But I had taken so many nutrients over the years and they never seemed to work. I could feel the raw juices and milk making me stronger. I was naïve and ignorant. I didn't realize that taking the right nutrients from a real health professional at the right time in the correct combinations and the right dosages was what could truly help the body.

Dede told me that people close to the Sufi Tradition had cured their diabetes by eating coconut oil regularly and prescribed such a course for me throughout the day for my blood sugar disorder. Within three weeks of eating lots of coconut oil daily, my condition was cured. I was able to eat white sugar for the first time in years with no problem.

I was also instructed to breathe in and out with a sacred Arabic word that meant "the cure." I am not sure if I can share the word itself because the breathing practice probably needs to be performed under the guidance of a teacher in case something unexpected happens.

The problem with this incredibly useful breathing technique was that my anxiety was so bad back in those days that just deeply breathing in and out caused me to feel as though I was going to hyperventilate, which was also caused by my chronic mouth breathing. I did my best, but it wasn't much. Since then, in recent years, I have used the same technique to cure myself of colds and various ailments.

I finished up the year at Ole Miss and moved back to whimsical Fairhope in the summer of 2005, eight hours southeast in a temporary rental. With my new diet, I needed to be somewhere I could buy raw milk and organic foods. I was tired of driving to Memphis for these—Oxford had nothing of the sort.

After a few more months of detoxifying, my body began to get much stronger. My body transformed into strong muscle, and people would stop me and ask if I played college football—a stark change from the scraggly pale freshman at Ole Miss just a few months earlier. During this time, Dede sent me a PDF file on Swedish Bitters and asked me to asked me to take them. I took them right away and got diarrhea. I now know this was a detox, but back then, it scared me and I stopped taking them. By this time, I was already washing my new clothes three or four times before I could wear them without them itching due to the formaldehyde sizing chemical manufacturers add to them. My skin felt like it was crawling due to this harmful element. Although I had seen some miraculous changes from my new healthy diet, I still felt so exhausted throughout most days.

Dede began sending energy, or *baraka*, to me long-distance throughout the day and at night. This energy was very profound and spiritual. It felt like I was in the presence of Love from the Creator when he sent me this energy. Also, around this time, Dede and I began to chat via MSN Messenger, which was a form of online chat.

One day, Dede informed me about thought field therapy (TFT) and emotional freedom therapy (EFT). He suggested I work with EFT Wizard Brad Yates in therapy sessions for my emotional issues. I read the book *Tapping the Healer Within* by Roger Callahan, the founder of TFT, and immediately began tapping with the algorithms. I also booked a session with Brad Yates right away. This was long before Brad had a YouTube channel with millions of views and was the leading authority on EFT. EFT is an emotional form of acupuncture that uses tapping with the fingers on various Chinese meridian points while

using positive affirmations according to the principles of neuro-linguistic programming (NLP) and
the forgiveness principles as detailed in *A Course in
Miracles* by Helen Schucman. TFT, on the other
hand, uses tapping on the meridian points in
specific patterns without affirmations, so it is a
simpler form of tapping, but equally as useful. I
found them both to be beneficial. In fact, Dr.
Mercola, a Chicago-based naturopath, has used
EFT for MCS patients with good results—some,
and I repeat some, MCS patients get cured
with EFT.

In my years being bedridden with Lyme, I had
done so much talk and dream therapy with Ken
Gilburth (my therapist from Mississippi) and that
had helped me. I had been an anxious child and
experimented with drugs my senior year in high
school. I had worked with Ken extensively on my
feelings for the girl who did not reciprocate my
love when we were thirteen. The Sufi Sheikh
Muzaffer Ozak (1916-1985) once said that when
someone has a very strong love for someone in the
world, it is really a love for the Beloved. Their
heart longs for a connection with God and is
ignited by a person in the world. I think that was
so true for me. That love began my spiritual search

for truth. Talk therapy had helped me in many ways to overcome my past, but I still had so many "issues" or "hang ups." I couldn't stop thinking about instances from my past that I regretted. I would turn them over and over in my mind, ruminating for hours. Maybe I had let a friend down or smoked a cigarette when I was fourteen behind my innocent parents' backs. I also still felt waves of regret about that girl when I was thirteen, and I didn't even like her anymore. I had written her a very sincere letter of apology while living in Asheville, North Carolina for my unusual behavior, which she had thanked me for. EFT had to be my answer.

After the first session with Brad, my perturbations about my past began to fade away rapidly. I also began using TFT every day when not in session with Brad for instances from my past that I kept ruminating over. Both worked like a charm—better than any talk therapy session I had ever had. I was finally feeling some emotional relief for the first time in years.

By this time, Dede had prescribed about two hours of so-called "Inner Work" every day for me in the form of exercises that were taken from the Sufi Tradition. According to the wisdom of the

Sufis, mankind has a small spiritual essence. Through exercises that involve the use of sound, head movements, repetitions (*zikhr*) in sacred language, and/or visualizing colors, man can clean the heart and activate the spiritual organs of perception (*latifas*) that lie dormant in their Being. But these exercises can only be done under the guidance of a Teaching Guide who knows the inner workings of the student and in the right context and at the correct time. They can never be applied haphazardly to anyone.

I was so happy to receive these inner exercises. I started them diligently, but couldn't keep them up with any consistency for two reasons: one, I was so tired all the time that I could not do them; and two, my neck hurt terribly when I would turn it during the exercises. This pained my heart deeply. After performing the exercise, I felt a deep sense of well-being and peace each time. I also had the sensation that I was very slightly drunk and of a collapse of time. One time, the time went by so fast while doing the exercise, it felt as if the longer time had only been a few minutes.

3

FEELING SENSITIVE

One cool fall day in October 2005, while chatting with Dede through Messenger, he suggested that I might move to St. Augustine, Florida, for my health and well-being, explaining that there was cosmic healing energy there that would serve my well-being and make my Inner Work very easy. I took a road trip there in my golden Chevrolet Tahoe with my mother and absolutely loved it—the oldest city in the United States, founded by Ponce de Leon in 1565. I could feel the energy there at once. It felt like I was in heaven. But I had always preferred cold coastal towns without much sun, so I asked Dede if there was anywhere similar along the east coast I could go. He replied that there was certainly nowhere else on the east coast with such energy, and that often in my life, I may have liked many things that were not good for me. I would reflect on this guidance many times in the years that followed.

I jumped all in and moved to St. Augustine. By this point, I was in regular phone contact with Aajonus Vonderplanitz, the raw food guru, about my diet and health. I still had regular detox from raw juices and after eating lots of raw fruit and raw fat. Not every day, but sometimes. I had noticed that when I would detox with the raw food, the smells of mainstream soaps and chemicals were strong and almost repugnant to me. For years, my throat, due to the eosinophilic esophagitis (EE), had felt like it was closing when I was around certain chemicals, like colognes and perfumes. Now, this began to make me afraid that they were toxic to me instead of mere allergies.

Dede told me that I should do as much inner work a day as I could for other members of our Institute long distance for my health and gave me a specific exercise for this, which involved sending energy from my heart to theirs. I did this with very good results, but my mental fatigue was a barrier too difficult to overcome sometimes. I would just lay there, flattened, wanting to do the work. Without the caffeine and nicotine, I no longer had any artificial stimulation to push me along like I had used for years.

Many times, when I wrote to Dede, he would say at the end of his reply, "Keep well, keep close, I am with you." After years of being on this strange health journey alone, it felt so good to have a true healer and spiritual mentor be there for me, inwardly and outwardly.

Dede advised I look into Reiki, an Eastern form of energy healing developed by a Japanese Buddhist named Mikao Usui (1865-1926). He said Reiki was very similar to the energy work in the Sufi Way. He said I would benefit by becoming an expert in it, and that I should have some sessions with an expert also. Eventually, I did become certified in Reiki and found everything Dede said about it to ring true.

I leased a temporary rental that backed up to the scenic intercoastal waterway. The unit was nice and well priced, right in the historic downtown, which I loved. St. Augustine was founded by Ponce de Leon in the sixteenth century while he was on his quest to find the fountain of youth, and the European-style architecture gave the place the feeling of another world—a lost and forgotten time where pirates and explorers roamed.

One day in the spring of 2006, the exterminator came around to spray all the units. He was standing there with my landlord, ready to enter my unit, when I opened the door. I knew talking them out of it was no use. I remember my father telling me how he had once told a bug guy that my mom was allergic to pesticides and the guy looked him square in the eye and said, "Sir, this stuff is so healthy, you could put it on your cereal and eat it in the morning." With my mom's reactions, and Vonderplanitz having already told me that household pesticides were no good, I was scared by this point. At the same time, I felt obliged to let the bug man in since this was a furnished vacation rental instead of my own apartment. So, I let them in to spray and went out casually for lunch.

While I was out, I called Vonderplanitz. He said, "Oh my goodness, everything in your apartment will be contaminated!" This freaked me out. I wondered if that was really possible. This was the first time I had thought about chemicals getting dispersed onto my things. It was a bad thought for me—a seed in my subconscious that would grow wicked fruit in time. I knew Aajonus had traveled all over the world to see patients, and he had recently been to workshops with clients of his in Finland and Antigua. There was no question he was 100 percent well physically, but he was unwell mentally when it came to chemicals. He was neurotic. I should have written Dede right away, but I didn't. Instead, I went back to my place and got into my mind. I was so nervous about chemicals at this point that I felt bad physically simply from the fear of them. Anxiety can be a very real physical ailment that can cause shortness of breath, temperature changes, fainting, muscle spasms, throat closures, and many other symptoms. I had already had real physical reactions to soaps, new clothes, perfumes, colognes, and cleansers at this point, but this was where the conditioning and warnings from Vonderplanitz combined with my anxiety disorder—which I had experienced since childhood—perhaps made the chemicals affect me worse than they would if my mindset was strong in being at peace and well in all circumstances.

I frantically packed my Chevrolet Tahoe with everything in the place and moved out as fast as I could to an old motor lodge up the street. It was the first time I would flee a place, and it established a pattern that would ruin my life for some years—a fight-or-flight mentality that meant I was never relaxed and okay. I didn't even think the exterminator had probably been there every month for ten years and I was doing quite fine in the place. I guess I assumed it was worse when he had just sprayed the pesticides than residual spray.

4

FIGHT OR FLIGHT

I canceled my rental place. It was a month to month pay-as-you-go apartment, so I wasn't out much money. I found another place to rent long term and asked the landlord if he would not paint or spray pesticides. He was a nice, laid-back guy from California who easily agreed. I was thrilled. However, the place wouldn't be available for a couple of months, and I couldn't find any affordable short-term rentals in the city, so I went back to Fairhope for the interim.

During this time, Dede recommended that I watch the hit movie *The Secret*, which was broadly about the law of attraction. This movie absolutely changed my life and the way I thought about myself and the world. The law of attraction states

that like attracts like, and that thoughts and feelings have frequencies that attract a corresponding
vibration or thing. Up until this point, I was still
watching horror movies sometimes. In spite of my
tapping and talk therapy, I still thought lots of
negative thoughts throughout the day. I was
already forming intentions and doing tapping
every day as part of my inner work, but after
watching *The Secret*, I stepped them up. I started
intending to be 100 percent well throughout the
day. But at this point, I wasn't clear enough inside
myself about my chemical sensitivities. I kept
thinking that something that feels so physical must
be physical in origin. No thought or feeling could
help turn it around. Nevertheless, I continued with
my intentions, doing them every day.

I also began studying HeartMath. This
involved breathing in through the heart while
feeling gratitude, a practice that could have a positive impact on heart rate variability levels—the
variation in between heartbeats. When HRV levels
are erratic, it indicates a highly stressed emotional
state, whereas stable and organized levels are an
indication of a calm, peaceful state. This form of
Heart Breathing gave me a sense of peace and
well-being. I bought the HeartMath software,

which came with an ear monitor that I hooked up to my computer. This software and earpiece allowed me to play games while monitoring my Heart Breathing. I also bought an EM Wave device that I placed my finger on. It read back positive HRV levels as green and negative ones as red through the finger. The idea was for the user to Heart Breathe and stay in the green zone.

I enjoyed my time back in Fairhope. It is a small, charming town. Fall football season was nice and cheerful. Everyone there was rooting for the University of Alabama Crimson Tide football team and the buzz of trips to Tuscaloosa, Alabama to see the games was in the air. Southern gentleman with good grooming and southern belles speckled the downtown, and it was always a pleasant place to be. A handmade chocolate store, an independent book and coffee store, friendly shopkeepers, and a high-end ladies' shoe store garnered the town a reputation as "The Carmel of the South." Carmel is a beautiful pleasant town on the ocean in Central California and Fairhope is similar because it is safe and you can walk everywhere.

Around this time, my erectile dysfunction (ED) reversed due to the energy (*baraka*) that Dede kept sending me long-distance, and I was able to be sexually active again. I fell in love with Debra, a girl from my hometown who lived up north; we mainly kept in touch via Facebook Messenger. I had hung out with Debra previously a few times in college in 2003—she also went to Ole Miss. She was one of the most beautiful women I had ever set eyes on at the time, and we had very good chemistry. She had asked if I was single and invited me to visit her in Knoxville, Tennessee. I was concerned about how my alternative diet would be perceived at this point—and now I had these ridiculous sensitivities and the occasional diarrhea from too many raw fruit juices—all leading to the conclusion that I needed to be stronger. So, I waited for things to change. I made assumptions about my circumstances and about her personality, and I didn't act. Looking back on it, a fun weekend full of intimacy with a beautiful loving woman would have gone a long way to getting me out of my silly head and into my Body and Being. At the same time, I didn't know much about her, and my opinions about her would change greatly for the worse as I got to know her better.

During this time, because of loneliness, I

started looking at pornography, which I always felt terrible about after watching. I just knew the pornography industry was so unhealthy. Around this time, Dede taught me about healthy tantra as described in Taoism, and introduced me to the books of Mantak Chia, a Thai Taoist master. Real tantra stated that the loss of semen gradually weakened a man, and the solution was to draw and circulate sexual energy up and around an energy channel in the body that ran from the head down to the feet in a circular fashion. Doing this allowed for multiple orgasms without losing semen or one's erection. One could have sex for many hours practicing this. I found this know-how to be very useful, and after some time, I stopped looking at pornography completely. My soul felt better.

After three months, the wait was over: it was time to move into my new place in St. Augustine. I arranged for my furniture to be moved there and set off on the ten-hour drive back to the European city on the intercoastal highway.

The day I arrived, a tragedy was waiting for me. I walked in to find my landlord touch up painting the walls with oil paint—something I was very sensitive to. We had agreed he would *not paint*. Oil paint is much stronger and off-gasses much worse than latex paint. It was even illegal in six states. I felt bad inside and I was determined not to move in. I realize multiple chemical sensitivities (MCS) has a very real physical component, but looking back, if I had just allowed my whole body to be completely at ease and at peace, and relaxed into my place while being centered in my being, I believe I could have stayed there.

I went to a coffee house the next day and talked to Dede, and he said the same thing: that I must find a way to live and be okay so the chemicals wouldn't bother me so much. By this point, I was so conditioned to think that paint and chemicals were toxic to me, despite all my law of attraction studies, I was petrified of them. And really, I was most scared of my throat closing because it was constricted a lot due to the eosinophilic esophagitis (EE)—which is medically incurable, by the way. Whenever I would eat any solid tough food like steak or chicken, I always had the sensation of it getting caught in my throat or maybe going down my windpipe. It was truly frightening.

A few days later, my furniture came—and man, I had great stuff. It was all my beautiful funky furniture from Asheville. But it wasn't great to me on this day, sitting there. No—it was worn out and scared.

I decided I couldn't stay there, even though I had already signed a year lease. The paint was too much. So I left my things there and stayed in a hotel for a week, which was hard also due to the chemical cleaning supplies they used. After that week, I now had my camping gear with me and decided to go to the state park on the ocean on Anastasia Island for two weeks. St. Augustine's beach is on an island across from the intercoastal highway. The state parks along the beach in that area of Florida are magnificent—pristine and untouched. But camping there was hot and diffi-cult. It rained three or four times a week, and I would have to move everything inside the tent or my car every time it rained.

I called the landlord after my camping foray and told him I wanted him to rent the unit to someone else and that I would pay the rent until then. He was baffled, but agreed. In the summer of 2006, I moved to my parents' home in Louisiana while I waited.

My parents' home in Covington was not ideal because it was very old and in a truly moist climate. The back area of the home where the guest bedrooms were had some mildew and light mold growing in the closets, and I never felt good back there, even before I got so bad off. Fortunately, I stayed in the living room on the sofa and close that back part of the house off because it had its own separate AC system.

5

SOMEWHERE ORGANIC

B rad Yates and Aajonus Vonderplanitz both lived in California, and I kept hearing how it was very organic from them and many other people. I knew the health food movement was born there with Paul Bragg, Arnold Tanney, and Jack LaLanne. I had been doing well in hotels for some odd reason. I would ask them not to spray air fresheners before I arrived. Every now and then, I would check in to one that I couldn't tolerate, but I did well in nicer ones. So my mom, Charme, and I decided to take a trip to the Carmel area of California on the Central Coast. I had grown up going there as a child, and it was heaven on earth to me. We used to stay at the Carmel Highlands Hotel and get in this big round hot tub, right in our room. The views swept down the jagged hillside to the rugged Pacific coast below. In that area, Monterey lies to the north and Big Sur to the south. In high school, I would carry around a copy of Henry Miller's *Big Sur* that I never even got around to reading, but it represented a place and a culture that I knew was out there somewhere, waiting to be discovered. That whole coast was full of the most magnificent nature I had ever seen.

I also wanted to see Vonderplanitz down south in Malibu for an iridology consult. Iridology is the study of the organs of the body through the color and discoloration in the iris. The eyes, this practice believes, are like a map of the whole body similar to the feet in Chinese foot reflexology points. Vonderplanitz had developed a highly sophisticated diagnostic system through his study of irises in order to prescribe certain foods based on toxicity present in certain areas of the body, as identified through the irises. Dede didn't seem to think it would help much, but told me it might be good to see Vonderplanitz regardless.

Mom and I set out to Malibu first and saw Vonderplanitz at his cool little home in the hills of Malibu up on Kanan Dune road. The place was like a hermit hideaway. Apparently, Fred Segal owned it and was one of Vonderplanitz's patients. He had many famous patients, apparently, and had even dated prominent British sixties model Twiggy back in his days as an actor. Vonderplanitz was sixty and his legs and arms were built like tree trunks. He was a short man and his eyes were the clearest, lightest blue color I have ever seen. They shone in the light like some rare gemstone. When I asked about them, he said he was born with dark brown eyes and it had taken many years of detox to get them blue.

I found the iridology process very interesting. With a macro lens on his Nikon D50, Vonderplanitz took brilliant photos of my eyes. He said I had large deposits of iron throughout my eyes, possibly from using iron cookware. It just so happens my mother used an iron skillet throughout my whole childhood, which is not rare at all. Vonderplanitz told me that most people got well from the chemical sensitivities in two weeks on his diet of eating whatever raw foods he allowed that they craved, but sometimes it took seven years. Seven years! I thought, my goodness, I can't wait that long. He showed me numerous patients' before-and-after iris photos. The changes in color from dark to light were unbelievable. One lady whose mother had been a crack addict had black eyes that turned almost completely blue after just a few years on the diet.

After seeing him, I looked at a few apartments in Santa Monica, which I just adored, but they all bothered me. The main symptoms I had were that my throat would close and I would become fatigued.

Vonderplanitz kept talking about how chemtrails were everywhere. I believed him, too—until I asked Dede about it and Dede said they were just contrails and water vapor, and all you had to do to disprove this ridiculous conspiracy theory was reflect on the cost of the whole operation—fueling airplanes and hiring pilots alone would cost trillions and trillions of dollars a year that the US government simply did not have. He said the US government was already borrowing money from China and Japan. Why would they spend money on this? That knowledge was a relief as I began to witness so many raw foodists and MCS people becoming so paranoid over this. It is truly incredible to me how someone can believe in something so much that they manifest physical reactions to something that is make believe as in the case of chemtrails.

From Santa Monica, mom and I traveled by car north to the charming quaint town of Carmel, California. I loved Carmel and felt like it was much more organic and earthy than Florida, but when it came to construction and rentals, people were still just blowing and going, using regular paint and pesticides. Even an organic-minded person would be using paints with VOCs (volatile organic compounds). I looked at several places to rent, but always felt bad in them. During this time, we looked at land for sale in the heavily forested mountain coastal village of Big Sur for me because I always felt best there. My parents loved it also. But it was very expensive and rural. The roads to the land we looked at snaked up mountains and were dangerous to drive on. We also took a scouting trip to the Big Island of Hawaii to look at houses. I kept thinking that if I just owned a place, I could control everything and be 100 percent well.

Mom and I returned home by car, stopping in Snowflake, Arizona to look at a chemical-free house for sale that I had found online. The place had been owned by a chemically sensitive lady who had lived there for years and was doing better. But the place was so isolated and when we met the woman, she still seemed so scared of life that the experience made me determined to be 100 percent well again.

I returned home defeated, but I did okay in my parent's house in Louisiana as long as I didn't stay in the back area. At least with them being very sympathetic and organically minded, I could control everything there. But I was still living at home. I was twenty-seven—too old to be living at home. What was I going to do with the rest of my life?

Around this time, I also learned from Dede about the use of color for health. Dede stated that like attracted like with color too, and that higher frequencies were attracted to lighter colors and lower frequencies were attracted to darker colors. At his suggestion, I began incorporating the color white into my wardrobe. He told me he had cured more people by having them change the color of their clothing and walls to white than any other thing he had ever prescribed. The white clothing seemed to help me in many ways to feel relaxed and protected. This is a very Eastern know-how that is little known in the West, by the way.

I decided to return to St. Augustine after living

at home for some months to try my l.   9

finding a new place, since I loved old

much. My previous place had rented, so I 1

to get out of the year lease. St. Augustii   was

romantic and reminded me of a Jimmy Buffett

song. I stayed in a two-story rental there, just one

block from Vilano Beach, with all-white walls and

light oak floors, owned by two very nice women.

One of the women was a massage therapist and

the other one owned a candle store downtown.

They were building a house next door and getting

ready to rent the whole house. I decided to rent it

from them when they agreed not to paint or spray

pesticides. Finally, I had found the perfect place.

The walls were even a nice, light color, there were

no chemicals, and the landlords were organic-

minded. The only problem was the A/C was moldy

when run, but they hadn't been using it, and I

figured I could live without that.

When the time came to move in, everything

seemed perfect. I had my furniture moved out of

storage and set up. I was so happy. The house was

nestled in the trees with an upstairs porch where I

could read or do inner work in the sun. A few

weeks after settling in, I decided that getting my

amalgam fillings removed could really help me to

do away with the chemical sensitivities completely. Dede and I talked pretty regularly via Messenger and email at that time (and rarely, on the phone) and he told me to go for it.

My mother had had her amalgam fillings removed in Louisiana a few years prior and said that the doctor was good, so instead of finding a local Florida doctor, I booked a session with my mom's and traveled home for the procedure. Before I left, Dede told me I needed to get tested for candidiasis because he felt certain I had it due to all the antibiotics from the Lyme treatment. Candidiasis is a chronic yeast infection that can get into the bloodstream and make a person feel very fatigued. In serious cases, it can also cause extreme chemical sensitivities. I felt he was right and wanted to do it. Dede was very wise and had unbelievable perception. The timing of his request seemed urgent to me. But now I had an appointment for the amalgam filling removal. I did not know what to do. Disregarding my better instinct, I figured I could get tested for the candidiasis as soon as I got back. That was the worst decision of my whole journey with MCS.

6

THE CURE

The amalgam filling removal was a total train wreck. I only had one of my three fillings removed. The dentist did not follow the protocol for proper amalgam removal: there was no vacuum in the office and the oxygen tube into my nose was not up high enough (nasal oxygen is used because the patient is asked to not breathe in during the drilling of the mercury filling as the vapors can be quite toxic when inhaled). Since childhood, I had been a mouth breather, and as such, I was breathing in through my mouth some during the procedure. If the oxygen into my nose had been high enough, it would have forced air up my nose as I can pull some oxygen in through my nose. Toward the end of the drilling, I began to feel terrible. I drove home and took a bath right away. I was so tired and weak. I relaxed over the next two weeks but felt more physically drained than normal. Even worse than that, I completely forgot about getting tested for candidiasis.

I did not return to that rental in St. Augustine yet—I needed to recover. Fortunately, my parents and I had the financial means to pay the rent every month, because the landlords would not let us out of our lease. But throwing money away like that was painful and traumatic for my mother, and that hurt my heart.

I had inherited some money when my grandfather passed away in 2001 and was able to repay my parents for all the antibiotics I received during my Lyme treatment, and I was able to cover most of my alternative health expenses, including groceries.

Finally, I gave up. Sometimes you reach a point in life where your ego just can't assert itself anymore. I had now prematurely moved out of three places. I thought I would just have to get well at my parents' house, and soon. It was the only place I did well. But I did not have my own area there, and eventually they had to replace the floor because the original wood was buckling. Underneath those floors was wet, moldy, cheap fiberglass insulation and replacing it would be expensive and very difficult. Furthermore, I had paid for and had very expensive HEPA filters from the Swedish company IQ Air installed on their air conditioning unit, but I did not perceive much of a change in the musky area in the back. We did have full house water filtration, which was wonderful—once you have MCS, clean water becomes an invaluable asset. At the time, my parents owned a vacation rental in Fairhope, Alabama and Dede suggested we move there for my convalescence. He suggested I keep my room highly oxygenated and ionized.

That house had been heavily sprayed with pesticides, so I hired a handyman to wipe the baseboards down with an organic degreaser. Seems neurotic now that I write it, but that was the world I lived in—the world of MCS, where you do bizarre things no matter the expense or the time it takes. I moved into that house with my mom, who stayed with me—dad drove out to see us on the weekends—and I did very well there. I was able to focus on curing myself since I no longer worried about dodging chemicals all the time, although I was still truly paranoid about the mosquito sprayer that came by the house every week or so. I would turn off the air conditioner when I heard the siren and wait until some time had passed before turning it back on. I paid to have a saltwater chlorinator put on our pool and I swam every day. I tapped for long periods with EFT and TFT. I also studied Spring Forest qi-gong at Dede's recommendation. Since meeting Dede, I never had met him in person, but we were in daily contact via email and chat. I also did many "micro-orbits" (as detailed by Mantak Chia) or circulating through visualization, a ball of golden light around an energy channel in the body that runs from the feet to the head in a circular manner around the whole body, lots of juicing, and many other things to get better.

Dede sent a missive to all members of our school about my health, asking them to do inner service work for me. For the next couple of days, I stayed in my room and was open to receiving this health. I could feel each soul's energy coming to me in different spots in the room. Some members were more advanced spiritually and their energy felt stronger, like Dede's. Some were weaker. I was so grateful for all of it.

Shortly after that, Dede empha

I needed to get tested for candidi

didn't wait. I immediately went t

I was determined to get over this illness.

came back positive and Dede advised I read Ed McCabe's *Flood Your Body with Oxygen*.

I read it and was amazed. Oxygen therapy had been used all over the world for years to treat illnesses of all kinds where traditional treatments had failed. Dede prescribed Cellfood, a stabilized oxygen and trace mineral supplement, at a dosage of eight drops three times daily, and told me to buy a polyatomic oxygen generator. I did both. I started with just one drop of Cellfood, which caused immediate diarrhea—but I felt so much better afterward. Over the next days of increasing the dose, I felt better and better. Then the Aranizer (the brand name of my oxygen generator) arrived and I would sit right next to it with it on high and breathe oxygen in very deeply. The Aranizer does not just produce O_2, but many forms of oxygen without the damaging effects that ozone causes when it binds in the air with toxins. Ozone (O_3), Dede explained, is healthy in the body and in water, but not in the air because when it binds with a toxin it creates a toxic byproduct. "Never use ozone air generator," he said. I had recently had a few phone consults with Master Lin, who developed Spring Forest qi-gong, and he told me that MCS was primarily an energetic blockage in the lungs. Master Lin told me that many people had been able to get over MCS by using his qi-gong technique every day. At the time, his technique was being studied by the Mayo Clinic in Minnesota for his incredible results with cancer. I find this point Lin made about the blockage in the lungs interesting because I was already doing better just days after I started using the Aranizer.

After a week, I was walking long distances down to the bay without fatigue, and I could be in public places with ease again. This was a miracle. Dede prescribed that I also buy Aranizer's water oxygenator, Iodoral (an iodine nutrient) supplement, and a nutrient called Transfer Factor made by 4Life. The Aranized water destroys anaerobic bacteria and yeast in the body that cannot live in the presence of oxygen, and iodine is a halogenic trace mineral (virtually nonexistent in the American diet) that the thyroid uses for all its functions. It was added to salt for the health of people in America. Transfer Factor, made from chicken egg yolks, seeks to recreate a substance that mothers give to their children through breast milk that acts like a map for the immune system to recognize intruders. I did everything Dede recommended, and also began taking magnesium daily—which was the first thing Dede had prescribed back in 2005 but which I never took until I was in Fairhope because of my fears. Everything Dede prescribed, he had me read and watch videos about, which were often on YouTube. He said this caused the elements and therapies to work more effectively because my mind would be working with them. And it is important to be informed about the things you're putting in your body in any case.

I had the Aranizer water generator delivered quickly. When I got it, I was like a kid on Christmas. I made the water immediately and drank a gallon a day of the good stuff. It had a wonderful taste. I started taking four 4Life Transfer Factor pills a day along with the iodine. Each new thing caused a little detox where I would have some mild diarrhea and a headache, but I was feeling stronger and better every day. My mindset was now on point 100 percent. I would test myself with chemicals—for example, using heavy industrial soap at a restaurant—with the mindset that I was going to be 100 percent well, and I was fine with the chemicals.

Within three to four weeks of starting the Cell-food, I was completely over my MCS and I decided to relax and let go. I felt well in my body for the first time since getting Lyme disease.

7

MY NEW LIFE

Shortly after taking the steps to cure myself in October 2008, I moved to Monterey, California, which was just north of Carmel along the Central Coast. I rented the place I wanted and didn't ask about paint or anything. My apartment was up on a beautiful little hill on Monte Vista Avenue, within walking distance of Whole Foods. I even used a shared laundry there that always had dryer sheets in the machine left over from other people, and even that did not bother me at all (they contain formaldehyde). I was free. At last!

It would take a little time and a stronger mindset before I could completely let go of all my fear of chemicals, but I did it. Now I go on construction sites as part of my job as a manager at my father's Palm Beach architectural office. And I even love the smell of fresh paint. I occasionally smoke a cigar, I enjoy wearing mainstream colognes, and I don't worry about bringing my own shampoo and soap when I stay at hotels.

While living in California, Dede suggested I take cayenne pepper throughout the day; this, combined with the earth energy in California at the time, cured my eosinophilic esophagitis throat condition also—a condition that my GI doctor in Monterey told me was incurable. My erectile dysfunction had returned before getting over MCS, and eventually, I tapped to a Brad Yates EFT video on sex issues that I found on YouTube for four days straight to eliminate that also.

Around that time, Dede sent out a wonderful YouTube video from the law of attraction teacher Joe Vitale on the Hawaiian spiritual practice of Ho'oponopono. He advised everyone in the Institute to practice this as much as possible for ourselves and others. The practice is one of radical forgiveness, like the kind taught in *A Course in Miracles*. This states that the world is a grand illusion and that everything in it is a manifestation of oneself, both good and bad things. Through making amends with the divine by using this radical forgiveness, one can help oneself and others. Joe had met a spiritual teacher, Dr. Hew Len, who practiced this ancient art of forgiveness. The idea was to take 100 percent responsibility for everything that showed up in one's life and to make amends with the divine through a prayer to God: "I love you. I am sorry. Please forgive me. Thank you." This mantra was said repeatedly for each issue. I began using this throughout the day with wonderful results. Instead of hating others for doing something I considered evil, I started asking for forgiveness. As Joe says, in everything I perceive, the good and bad, the one common denominator is me. I am always there.

8

FREEDOM

I moved around a bit out West, just for fun, between 2009 and 2012. In October 2012, circumstances brought me back to Louisiana.

I lived a good, simple life in my one-bedroom apartment on the north shore of Louisiana for five years with no more MCS symptoms. I made many good friends in that area and in New Orleans—New Orleans was wonderful for me because there was killer live music, soulful creole food, and lots to do. During this time, I was very active with NAMI—the National Alliance on Mental Illness—and made many good contacts there. Over the years, after trying many natural remedies including St. John's Wort, amino acids, Sam-E, Bach flower remedies, etc., I finally found two medicines for my mental health that I take daily with truly spectacular results: the first, Latuda, is for my thought disorder (and is also good for bipolar); the second is Lexapro, for anxiety.

After self-publishing my first 550-page novel, *The Opaque Stones* in 2014 which I wrote in California, I got the perfect job doing social media, website work, and public relations (skills Dede had taught me while living out West) for my father's architectural firm where I have been working since 2015. My job requires quite frequent travel, which I do with no issues, mentally or physically. I have a new Grand Design Reflection RV that I take all over America on vacation. In 2018, I took it with me to go fly-fishing in New Mexico and Colorado, while working long-distance for our firm.

In July 2018, I met my wonderful Thai wife, Wiphawan Tate, on an online dating site. Her name means "radiance" in Thai and she truly does radiate love and kindness—and she's the best cook ever. We are now very happily married and deeply in love. This year, I bought a new condo in southeast Florida. I had it completely painted with no problems, I am happy to say. And I am so happy also to say that I don't care about ever moving to a new city again because there is nothing to escape from—anymore.

9

BEING AT EASE

Over the five years of living in my Louisiana apartment, I remained in close contact with Sufi Teachers. I learned from them to Be Still and To Be. I kept wanting to move back to Florida or California, but I told myself, "No, not yet. Let's just be right here, right now, in this moment. Everything you need is in this moment. God is in the now."

I quit coffee for many years until I found the right medication and learned to be at peace. Now I have a coffee every now and then, and I even smoke a cigar sometimes. I have learned to tolerate wearing mainstream colognes because their smells lift my whole well-being—in fact, I have heard of some cases of MCS being cured from aromatherapy alone. Fragrances can have a powerful effect on the body and being. I am not advocating anyone go out and buy a new mainstream cologne after reading this if they have chemical sensitivities, nor I am advocating smoking. I have been juicing now almost daily for twelve years. I have gotten rid of every trace of candidiasis from my system. I have mastered the art of being well and at peace around chemicals also. My mental health is very high these days. What I am saying now to you is that anything is possible.

I don't know what causes MCS. Dede said in my case, I should not go to the famous Rhea Clinic in Dallas that specializes in treating people with chemical sensitivities. I have heard of people who got well from going there, and others who didn't have any change. Perhaps Dede knew my chemical sensitivities were caused by candidiasis because of all the antibiotics I was given. I now know Candida was the true cause of my sensitivities, and my anxiety condition made it all the worse. I don't know that your situation is the same.

Mindset is everything. Some days in Louisiana, I would meditate for a very long time with the goal being to stop my thoughts from flowing. When the mind is calm and uncluttered, you can perceive things clearly. I so wish I had just stopped to breathe when I rented that first place in St. Augustine. I wish I hadn't listened to all of Aajonus's paranoid, grandiose fears about chemicals, even though he helped me in many other ways. When ruminations and rapid anxious thoughts are flowing, you don't always know what to do, and a thought is a very powerful thing. When a person starts to think the pesticides are going to make their throat close, their mind has already started telling the throat to close—because the body obeys commands from the thoughts, and according to the law of attraction, what we think, we will manifest.

Everybody I met when I had MCS—and there were quite a few—dreamed about owning a perfectly clear house on the ocean where they had strong, healthy negatively charged ionized air blowing in their windows all the time. That is truly a wonderful thing, and I wish everybody could have that. But what is the true cost? Can you afford it? Most people can't. If you can't afford it now but you still want it, tack it on your vision board, but forget about it completely in terms of your well-being strategy. You must try to get 100 percent well in all situations, not only once you are in that house on the ocean—that is a "boy in the bubble" mindset where you have to be isolated from the world in order to be well. Even if you have that house, you won't be well in the world as it is now. The world we live in is the product of the Chemical Revolution, which followed the Industrial Revolution. We are now in the Technological Revolution. If you want to have a good, simple life, you need to set your mindset to being 100 percent okay and at ease around all chemicals in the world. By this, I don't mean to expose yourself unnecessarily to any excessive amount of chemicals. I mean you must be well with the regular cleaning chemicals, air fresheners, and bug sprays that are being used out in the world by most people and in most places.

One thing I did to get 100 percent over MCS was to stop blaming people. I used to blame Monsanto and Tide and all these chemical companies for my problems. That's being a victim. You must take responsibility for your health where you are, and go from there. That's the only way you can proceed. Be at cause instead of at effect.

HOW TO SUCCEED

In this chapter, I am going to summarize what I think a person suffering from MCS should start out doing.

The first thing a person should do is to *relax*, be at peace and *at ease*, and make efforts in this direction throughout the day. If you drink coffee and it causes your mind to race, you should stop it *immediately*. Switch to green tea. If that causes anxiety, you are better off without caffeine until you learn to be at peace. Watch the movie *The Secret* many times. Review the recommended reading section here. The most useful mindset books include *The Key* by Joe Vitale, *Happy for No Reason* by Marci Shimoff, and *Tapping the Healer Within* by Roger

Callahan. Tap with EFT and TFT as much as
possible for chemicals. Brad Yates has hundreds of
YouTube videos on EFT worth tapping to.

It is best to proceed without thinking primarily
about chemical toxicity. Disease cannot live in an
alkaline body; therefore, whatever condition a
person has, they would be wise to alkalinize as
much as possible with the food they eat. Some
foods are alkaline and some are acidic.
Hippocrates said, "Let food be thy medicine." That
is so true.

The most alkalinizing foods on the planet are
organic raw fruit and vegetable juices. Start slowly
and work up. I don't juice kale, and use only small
amounts of ginger because these foods are very
strong and cause a rapid detox. Many bottled raw
juices sold at Whole Foods have too much ginger
in them. In my juices, I use lots of apples, celery,
carrots, grapes, cucumbers, and some parsley to
make a green juice. Also, consume lots of salads
full of raw vegetables like tomatoes and cucumbers. One can test one's urine alkalinity by buying
pH paper at health food stores. From 1 to 6.9 is
acidic, neutral or balanced at 7 and from 7 upwards
is alkaline on a scale of 14. pH should be 7.2 to 7.4

for cellular health to be present. Measure urine or saliva. Remember, pH paper will show values 0.8 lower than what is actually present in your body, so if the pH paper reads 6.4 to 6.6 you will be at healthy alkaline levels. Raw apple cider vinegar with "the mother" is one of the most alkalinizing foods on the planet and blackstrap molasses is also very good due to the abundant iron and potassium.

All raw foods, like all good medicinals, cause detoxification.

I would also encourage anyone with sensitivities to get tested for candidiasis as soon as possible. This is so important because it is an easy thing to cure and get over. Many people with MCS feel they have a toxicity issue and need to detoxify. That may be the case in some situations, but it's best to rule out candidiasis to start with because it causes such extreme chemical sensitivities. I put this test off against Dede's advice because I kept thinking in terms of the detox model of MCS as opposed to a bug model. I personally did some parasite and liver cleanses from Hulda Clark's work along the way, but never had any change from this, although it seems to be very useful for certain illnesses.

Hulda Clark is famous for writing a book called *The Cure for All Diseases* about how parasites that feed on chemicals in the human body are the root cause of all diseases. She recommends killing them through an electric frequency with a zapper and taking various herbal remedies to destroy them. There is no evidence I know of that parasites can cause chemical sensitivities per se, although they may cause many other strange symptoms. Getting rid of candidiasis, on the other hand, quickly cured me of MCS.

Here are some other things one may try and do slowly, gradually adding in one thing at a time so as not to overwhelm the body—always while using and maintaining the intention to be 100 percent well.

Buy or obtain the best water you can find and place it in a Vitalizer Plus machine, which creates structured water—this is water that is hexagonal in nature. There is a lot of research out now about the structure and nature of water. Spring water from high mountain lakes and streams has a hexagonal structure that is lost in our modern water because of pipes that run in straight lines and chemicals used by municipalities. One can also add a hydrogen capsule to a pitcher of hexagonal water because almost all water is now deficient in hydrogen due to sanitization and source of the water. Hydrogen is the most powerful antioxidant in the world. Real structured and hydrogenated water, like all good medicinals and raw food, causes detoxification. It may be that people with MCS often—as I did—mistake detoxification as a symptom for the problem. One should proceed slowly and carefully, being fully attuned to what is a detox and what isn't.

Everyone would do well to get fifteen minutes of sun a day, minimum. If you live in an overcast climate like Seattle, obtain a near-infrared light to use when the sun is not present. The human body needs sufficient vitamin D and heat from the sun every day to maintain health.

Using some form of stabilized oxygen every day, preferably Cellfood, does wonders for the body. I had IV ozone injected into my bloodstream after I got well every day for three weeks just because I thought it would cure my eosinophilic esophagitis. Some people do very well on ozone and have amazing results—and I must admit, I did feel truly well on it—but it's very expensive (I spent $30,000 of my own savings on it!) and it's no substitute for getting a little oxygen every single day in your system for many months through a cheap nutrient like Cellfood. I believe it is better for certain conditions to receive oxygen daily and consistently for a long time than to receive it in more intense bursts for a short time. For other conditions, IV ozone may be more beneficial. People who are worried about nutrients packaged in plastic bottles like Cellfood need to relax and reflect deeply on that, in my opinion. You may never be able to proceed with that mindset. I have tried Health Force's Oxygen Elements, which is bottled in glass, and find Cellfood to be superior.

When you wake up every morning, make a list of your intentions—the things you intend to happen in your life. Also make a separate list of everything you are grateful for. Gratitude is the key to success in life. There is always something to be grateful for: a pair of shoes, daylight, being alive, and having woken up after a night of sleep, etc.

Look deeply into the following nutrients: magnesium, CoQ10, vitamin C, Iodoral, 4Life's Transfer Factor, and Sun Chlorella. Have a chiropractor skilled in applied kinesiology test you for these or learn how to test yourself online. Sun Chlorella is a potent detoxifier, so if you are concerned about a toxic burden, look closely into this in particular. It is one of the best superfoods on the planet and studies show that it can even detoxify mercury and other heavy metals from the body.

Wear only clothing made of natural fibers like silk, cotton, wool and cashmere. If you like workout clothes, look into Tasc which makes cotton and bamboo blended clothes that wick moisture and breathe well.

In addition to Cellfood, research polyatomic oxygen generators like the Aranizer I used to cure my MCS. Aranizer was bought by Royal Knight Air Purifiers some years ago, and I don't know if they are still in business anymore, though you can probably still buy used Aranizers online. You might also talk to a health professional about trying Aranized water as I did.

Turkish baths, saunas, and ozone saunas can all be very good for detox also.

If you decide to have your amalgam tooth fillings removed, do so only when you are strong, and go to a dentist who is truly skilled and knowledgeable in mercury removal. After and before, take Jon Barron's Metal Magic, which is a mixture of cilantro and chlorella extract. I recently had my remaining two fillings removed with no problems at all, and I bought six bottles of Metal Magic for it.

Find a spiritual practice, such as the Sufi Way, Buddhism, the Kinslow System, or Ho'oponopono, and engage with it with all your being.

Wishing you all a lifetime of health, abundance, joy, and peace.

RECOMMENDED READING

Alt, Carol. *Eating in the Raw: A Beginner's Guide to Getting Slimmer, Feeling Healthier, and Looking Younger the Raw-Food Way*. New York: Clarkson Potter, 2004.

Barron, Jon. *Lessons from the Miracle Doctors*. Laguna Beach, CA: Basic Health Publications, 2008.

Byrne, Rhonda. *The Secret*. New York: Atria Books, 2006.

Callahan, Roger, and Richard Trubo. *Tapping the Healer Within: Using Thought Field Therapy to*

Instantly Conquer Your Fears, Anxieties, and Emotional Distress. New York: McGraw Hill, 2001.

Campbell, T. Colin, and Thomas M. Campbell II. *The China Study: The Most Comprehensive Study of Nutrition Ever Conducted and the Startling Implications for Diet, Weight Loss, and Long-Term Health.* Dallas, TX: BenBella Books, 2006.

Gallo, Fred, and Harry Vincenzi. *Energy Tapping.* Oakland, CA: New Harbinger Publications, 2000.

Kinslow, Frank. *The Secret of Instant Healing.* Hay House, 2011.

Kinslow, Frank. *EuFeeling!: The Art of Creating Inner Peace and Outer Prosperity.* Carlsbad, CA: Hay House, 2012.

Pratt, Stephen, and Kathy Matthews. *SuperFoods Rx: Fourteen Foods That Will Change Your Life.* New York: HarperCollins, 2004.

Vitale, Joe. *The Key: The Missing Secret for Attracting Anything You Want.* Hoboken, NJ: John Wiley & Sons, 2008.

Vonderplanitz, Aajonus. *We Want to Live.* Carnellian Bay Castle Press, 1997.

ONE-ON-ONE SESSIONS

I will be booking one-on-one coaching sessions for people with Multiple Chemical Sensitivities who have read my books and feel they would benefit from my guidance. If you are interested in having such a session, contact me at:

windstream80@gmail.com

Please list your full name, age, location, and symptoms. It is a requirement that you have read this whole book. I will be working on donations, which you can provide via my PayPal address of the same email after each session.

NOTES

1. Lyme Disease

1. The day I arrived in Asheville, I got the call that my grand-father Irwin Tate had died of a heart attack at seventy-one years of age. He had a bad heart valve and had been taking Viagra to be sexually active with his younger girlfriend. His death had a profound effect on me as he had tried so hard to help me get well.

ABOUT THE AUTHOR

Duke Tate was born in Mississippi where he grew up surrounded by an age-old tradition of story-telling common to the deep South. He currently lives in Southeast Florida where he enjoys fishing, surfing, cooking Asian food and reading. This is his first book.

You can view his YouTube channel here and his author website here.

amazon.com/Duke-Tate

goodreads.com/9784192.Duke_Tate

facebook.com/duketateauthor

twitter.com/duke_tate

ALSO BY DUKE TATE

The Opaque Stones

The Alchemy of Architecture: Memories and Insights
from Ken Tate

Coming Soon:

Big John and the Fortune Teller

Ken Tate in Black and White

Gifts from a Guide: Life Hacks from a Spiritual Teacher

The Sun is Always Shining in Paradise: Learning to
Live in the Now

Printed in Poland
by Amazon Fulfillment
Poland Sp. z o.o., Wrocław

60764814R00063